W9-BXY-941

Understanding Genetics™

Introduction to Genetics

Carol Hand

ROSEN
PUBLISHING®

New York

To the memory of I.R.E., with thanks for the genes

Published in 2011 by The Rosen Publishing Group, Inc.
29 East 21st Street, New York, NY 10010

Library of Congress Cataloging-in-Publication Data

Hand, Carol, 1945–
Introduction to genetics / Carol Hand.—1st ed.
    p. cm.—(Understanding genetics)
Includes bibliographical references and index.
ISBN 978-1-4358-9531-7 (library binding)
1. Genetics—Juvenile literature. 2. Genes—Juvenile literature. I. Title.
QH437.5H36 2010
576.5—dc22

2009040364

Manufactured in the United States of America

CPSIA Compliance Information: Batch #S10YA: For further information, contact Rosen Publishing, New York, New York, at 1-800-237-9932

On the cover: DNA's four nitrogenous bases always pair the same way, binding the strands together. Their sequence down the strands determines the content of our genes, which determines who we are.

Contents

Introduction

Why are there so many kinds of plants and animals in the world? Why do some twins look alike and others look different? How can two brown-eyed parents have a blue-eyed baby? People have been asking questions like these for thousands of years. These types of questions—and the search for their answers—eventually led to the development of a new science. This science is called genetics.

Genetics is the study of heredity, or the passing of traits from one generation to the next. Geneticists figure out how traits are inherited. They determine how likely a trait is to show up in the next generation. Will all offspring (children) have it? One-half? One out of four? The field of genetics covers anything to do with genes, the tiny units inside cells that make heredity possible. Genes are parts of a molecule of DNA, so genetics is also about DNA.

Why does genetics matter? First, genetics is essential in agriculture. The incredible variety of healthy foods in our supermarkets is there because of genetics. Second, we need genetics to understand health and disease. Which diseases are inherited and how? How likely is it that a child will inherit a condition from a parent or grandparent? Can scientists "fix" a gene so that future generations will not inherit the disease? With today's genetic techniques, there can

Identical twins are formed when one egg is fertilized and then divides to form two embryos. Despite identical DNA, these twins are unique individuals because their environments differ slightly.

be answers to these questions. Scientists are now using genetics to save endangered species and clean up polluted areas. They're even using genetics to solve crimes. More applications for genetics are discovered all the time.

CHAPTER one

The Road to Mendel's Garden

Humans have been tinkering with nature for thousands of years. About ten thousand years ago, groups of people gave up the hunting-gathering lifestyle and settled down. They began to grow and store food. These early farmers domesticated crops and animals for food. They brought animals in from the wild and gave them food and shelter. They planted fields of grain and gardens of vegetables. Early farmers tried to improve their plants and animals by selective breeding. They selected the parents of each new generation. They chose grains with the fullest heads. They chose cattle and goats that produced the most milk. They hoped the parents would pass these chosen characteristics on to new generations.

For centuries, no one understood exactly how parents' traits were passed on to their offspring. Farmers just selected good parents and hoped for the best. Usually, the babies had the desired traits—but not always. Farmers did not understand why traits sometimes showed up in the next generation and other times didn't.

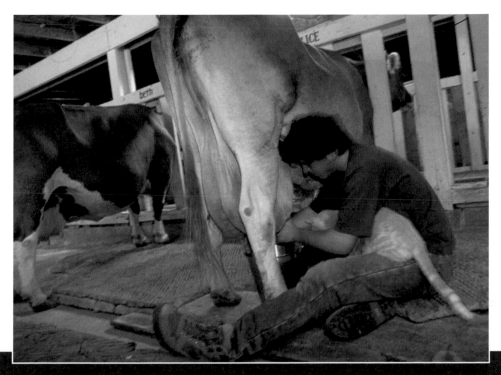

Dairy cattle have been selectively bred for high milk production. Before genetic engineering, selective breeding of certain breeds of cattle was the only method for genetically improving livestock.

Genetics Before Mendel

About 400 BCE, the Greek philosopher Hippocrates suggested that seeds or particles produced in the bodies of both parents were blended. He thought this explained why a child showed characteristics of both parents. Aristotle, another Greek philosopher, did not agree. He said it could not be true because some children do not resemble their parents. But Aristotle's own explanation said much the same thing. He thought heredity occurred when fluids from both parents' bodies were mixed.

Hippocrates and Aristotle simply thought about how heredity occurred. They did not make controlled observations, do experiments, or collect data. They had no real evidence to back up their ideas. They were basically guessing. Nevertheless, people accepted the idea of "blending inheritance" for more than two thousand years.

In the 1700s and 1800s, a few people developed another, rather strange idea of heredity called preformation. These people thought future generations were already fully made within the sex cells. They thought smaller and smaller organisms fit inside each existing organism, like tiny nested dolls. Some people, using early microscopes, were convinced that they could actually see tiny complete "men" inside human sperm cells!

Darwin, Evolution, and the Dawn of Genetics

During the nineteenth century, science changed forever. Instead of guessing, two men separately collected and analyzed large amounts of data. They developed theories to explain what they saw. These two scientists never worked together. They never even met. They worked in different countries and in different fields of science. But after they died, other scientists connected their data and ideas. Together, their ideas formed the basis of modern genetics. One of these men was Charles Darwin, who developed the theory of evolution. The other was Gregor Mendel, now known as the "father of genetics."

Darwin was a naturalist and geologist. From 1831 to 1836, he was the naturalist aboard the British ship HMS *Beagle*. During this voyage around South America, Darwin collected plants, animals, and fossils at every stop. He recorded detailed observations of their structures and habitats. He noticed that organisms varied

Charles Darwin (1809–1882). Darwin's theory of evolution by natural selection explains the diversity of life and unifies concepts throughout the field of biology. His book On the Origin of Species *was published in 1859.*

by habitat. For example, South American plants and animals looked different from the same types in Europe. Most people at the time believed that life on Earth had never changed. Darwin began to question this belief. His observations led him to think that life constantly changed, or evolved. His examinations of living things showed that they were adapted to their environments. His observations of fossils suggested that new species could evolve over very long periods of time.

Darwin continued to observe nature for many years after he returned to England. He figured out patterns in his data and tried to explain them. Finally, in 1859, he published a book, *On the Origin of Species*, which described his theory of evolution. Although another naturalist named Alfred Russel Wallace independently developed the same theory, it bears Darwin's name because Darwin published his observations and theory before Wallace did. Both men backed up this theory with many years' worth of evidence. The theory bears Darwin's name because he did a great deal more research.

Evolution by Natural Selection

Darwin's theory of evolution deals with changes within populations. A population is a group of organisms of the same species that live in the same place. Evolution describes changes to populations over long periods of time. The changes are very tiny, but they occur over many generations. Darwin's theory proposes a process by which these changes occur.

A theory is a well-tested, evidence-based explanation of how something happens. It describes a process by which all the facts came to be. Darwin's theory describes how populations adapt, or change, as their environment changes through a process called natural selection. Natural selection relies on two factors. One factor is the presence of inherited variations, or differences, which all organisms have. These variations are obvious in family members.

They look similar, and you can tell they are related. But they are not identical. The differences are inherited variations. The other factor is stress caused by the environment. Environmental stress might be the lack of food or the presence of competing species or predators. It might also be a change in climate.

According to Darwin, all species undergo a "struggle for existence." For example, what if some plants in a population withstand hot, dry conditions better than others? In hot, dry years, these plants still reproduce and leave many new plants to form the next generation. Plants that die more quickly in such weather leave fewer offspring. The next generation has more plants that can survive these conditions. If the weather stays hot and dry for many years, the "hot, dry" trait builds up. Plants that don't have it decrease in number. If most years are mild, both traits will be present in more equal numbers.

The Legacy of Darwin and Mendel

Charles Darwin and Gregor Mendel changed science forever. Darwin proved that populations and species adapt. Mendel proved that these adaptations are passed from generation to generation in a precise, predictable way.

Darwin was a master of observation. He observed nature to answer specific questions. Because any observation might be important, he also recorded dates, times, locations, and weather conditions—any factor that might affect organisms. Darwin knew it was important to continue observations for long time periods. He tried to fit all his data into meaningful patterns, and he developed theories to fit them.

Mendel was also an excellent observer. But Mendel did more. He conducted experiments and analyzed them mathematically. He applied physics techniques to the study of biology. Mendel's precise experiments showed patterns in his data that led to the laws of genetics.

Darwin's theory began to explain heredity. His observations described changes in traits through generations and convinced him that natural selection occurred in populations. But he could not explain how traits were transferred between individual organisms. Someone had to answer this question before other scientists would accept natural selection. Darwin tried to explain it by pangenesis, or "whole birth." He suggested body cells shed tiny pieces called gemmules, which collected in reproductive organs and helped determine the offspring's characteristics. But Darwin had no evidence for pangenesis. How natural selection happened remained a puzzle.

One missing piece of Darwin's puzzle was published in 1866, only seven years after his own work. This paper, "Experiments in Plant Hybridization," was by an Augustinian friar named Gregor Mendel. Mendel gave evidence and proposed a method for passing information about traits from parent to child.

Gregor Mendel: The Father of Genetics

The future father of genetics was born on July 22, 1822, in Heinzendorf, Austria, a village that is now part of the Czech Republic. In 1843, Johann Mendel entered the Abbey of St. Thomas in Brünn and took the name "Gregor." The Abbey was a wonderful place to learn. It had scientific instruments, a large botanical collection, and a library of several thousand books. It also had extensive gardens. The friars were teachers, university professors, and researchers. They encouraged Mendel's interest in science. In 1851, the abbot sent Mendel to the University of Vienna. There, he studied physics and botany. Physics taught him to use experiments and mathematics. Botany stimulated his interest in plant variation and inheritance.

When he returned to the monastery, Mendel taught physics. But he spent most of his time in the monastery gardens. From

Gregor Mendel (1822–1884). After Mendel's death, his successor burned all original notes on his inheritance experiments. Fortunately, Mendel's one published paper summarized his most important data.

1856 to 1865, he conducted studies of inheritance in garden peas. Unfortunately, Mendel's one published paper was ignored during his lifetime. It was not rediscovered until 1900, sixteen years after his death.

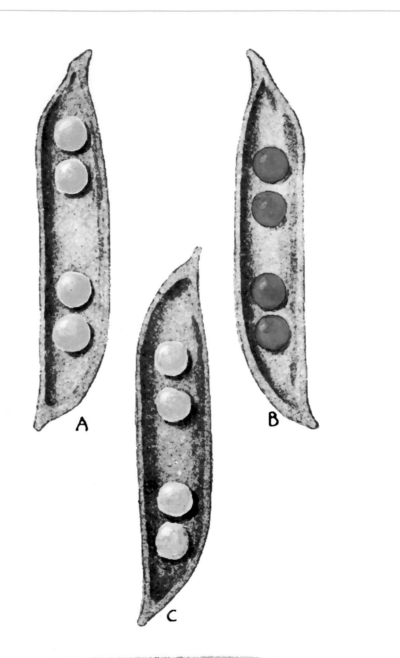

When Mendel crossed paired traits, such as yellow and green seeds, he counted every pea produced. These counts helped him develop the laws of genetics.

Mendel's Peas

Mendel needed a test species to show inheritance patterns. He chose garden peas because they had many traits that were present in two—and only two—forms. These "either-or" traits were easy to distinguish. Seeds were either yellow or green. Plant stems were either long or short. Mendel studied seven pairs of these simple traits.

Also, peas can self-fertilize because the flowers contain both male and female parts. New plants form when a plant's pollen fertilizes its own egg cells. Mendel studied only pea plants that "bred true." That is, the offspring of self-fertilized plants always looked exactly like their parents. This meant Mendel could be sure of the ancestry of each plant.

Mendel also chose peas because he could pollinate them by hand. First, he removed the stamens from a flower before it produced pollen. This prevented the plant from self-pollinating. Then he used a small paintbrush to dust mature pollen from another plant onto the flower. This cross-pollination produced hybrid plants.

For eight years, Mendel grew and tested between twenty-eight thousand and thirty thousand pea plants. He made sure all pea varieties were true-breeding by counting the offspring from every cross. Then he began cross-pollinating plants with specific traits. First, he tested one trait at a time. Later, he tested combinations of two and three traits. By carefully counting the offspring of thousands of crosses, Mendel collected a wealth of data.

CHAPTER two

Mendel's Laws of Inheritance

Gregor Mendel tested seven "either-or" traits in garden peas. He carefully analyzed the results from thousands of crosses, calculating ratios of traits in the offspring. From these results, he developed three laws of inheritance. Mendel deduced both the first and second laws from monohybrid crosses, or crosses testing one trait at a time. More complex dihybrid and trihybrid crosses led to the third law. Mendel's crosses and his thought processes are complicated. They must be followed step-by-step.

Monohybrid Crosses

First, Mendel reasoned that peas inherited two "factors," one from each parent, which determined a trait. He tested this hypothesis by doing monohybrid crosses. For example, he crossed a plant that bred true for yellow seeds with one that bred true for green seeds. These two plants were the mother and father in his cross. They were the first (parent) generation. This cross produced a second generation with all yellow seeds. The yellow-seed trait is dominant because it

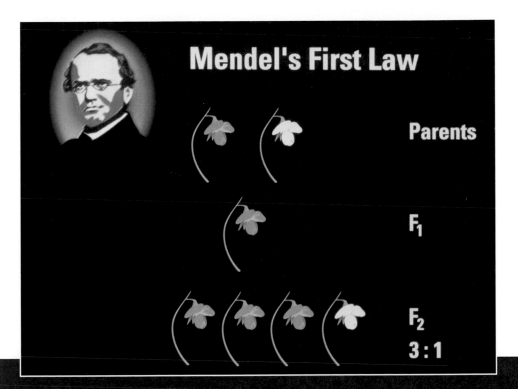

Mendel's First Law

Parents

F₁

F₂

3 : 1

The 3:1 ratio of violet to white flowers in the third generation shows that violet is dominant. White flowers appeared one-fourth of the time, only when two recessive alleles were paired.

completely masks the presence of the green-seed trait. The masked form (green seeds) is recessive.

But the recessive trait did not disappear. Mendel proved it still existed by allowing members of the second generation to self-fertilize. This produced a third generation in which one-fourth of the seeds were green.

Mendel's Results

What Mendel called factors are now called genes. The two forms of each gene—the "either-or" factors, such as yellow or green seeds— are called alleles of the gene.

In Mendel's data, there are three times as many dominant plants as recessive plants. The larger the number of plants tested, the closer the ratio is to 3:1. This is because large sample sizes help even out random variations. Mendel knew he needed large sample sizes for accurate results.

Mendel's Conclusions

The third generation had both pure yellow and pure green seeds. There were no blended forms. That is, crosses of yellow and green seeds did not produce yellowish-green or greenish-yellow seeds. The same held true for all traits tested. The fact that traits from both parents showed up unchanged in the third generation supported Mendel's hypothesis. This hypothesis became known as the theory of particulate inheritance, which says that traits are determined by factors (genes) that pass unchanged from generation to generation. This conclusion was a breakthrough in the study of inheritance. It disproved the old idea of "blending inheritance."

During Mendel's time, people knew nothing about cell structures that determined inheritance. Still, Mendel deduced what happened inside the cell. He reasoned that the two separate factors sorted randomly in each parent and entered the sex cells. In peas, the egg and pollen grain would each contribute one factor to determine a trait such as seed color. If each second-generation parent produced equal numbers of each type of sex cell (for example, green-seed and yellow-seed cells), there was an equal chance of the offspring receiving either type. From these data, Mendel deduced the law of segregation. This second law states that pairs of factors (alleles) segregate randomly and unchanged into separate sex cells.

Mendel's research led to many new discoveries. Some scientists determined patterns of inheritance in other species and figured out more complex types of inheritance. Others studied cell structure,

This garden at the Abbey of St. Thomas in Brünn, Austria-Hungary (now Brno, Czech Republic), was the site of Mendel's experiments on inheritance in the garden pea.

discovered chromosomes, and described cell reproduction and division. Still others tracked down the exact nature of Mendel's "factors," the genetic material now known as DNA.

The Language of Genetics

Mendel crossed visible traits, or phenotypes, and counted the different phenotypes that appeared in the offspring. From his data, he deduced the combination of alleles producing each phenotype, which is called the genotype. The genotype is hidden inside the cell's DNA.

Scientists use a shorthand way to describe alleles in genotypes. A capital letter stands for the dominant allele. For example, *Y* stands for yellow seeds. The lowercase *y* stands for the recessive allele of the same gene, such as green seeds. Each parent gives one allele— *Y* or *y*—to each offspring. So offspring have one allele from each parent to make a pair for each trait.

Some genotypes have two alleles of the same type. If both alleles are either dominant (*YY*) or recessive (*yy*), they are called homozygous genotypes. Other genotypes (*Yy*) have one recessive and one dominant allele. These are called heterozygous genotypes.

The Punnett Square

Reginald Crandall Punnett (1875–1967), an English geneticist, developed the Punnett square. This diagram can predict outcomes of crosses. It illustrates the results of a cross by showing all possible genotype combinations. It shows how recessive traits persist in a population. It also shows how different alleles segregate during sex cell formation and regroup in offspring.

This Punnett square shows a monohybrid cross:

Alleles in Sperm

		Y	y
	Y	YY	Yy
Alleles in Eggs	y	Yy	yy

The *Y* and *y* alleles across the top are yellow and green alleles that the sperm in the pollen grain from a heterozygous plant can donate. The *Y* and *y* alleles on the left side are possible alleles from the egg. The four squares inside the box show how the heterozygous parents' alleles can pair at fertilization. These pairs represent the only four possible combinations of these two alleles.

A monohybrid cross of two heterozygous parents can produce three possible genotypes in the next generation. A *YY* offspring receives a dominant allele from each parent and has a yellow phenotype. All this plant's sex cells will have the dominant *Y* allele. A *Yy* offspring has one dominant and one recessive allele. Yellow is dominant over green, so the green allele is masked and *Yy* genotypes also have yellow phenotypes. It makes no difference that the dominant *Y* allele came from the mother in one *Yy* offspring and from the father in the other. Half the sex cells produced by these plants will contain the *Y* allele. The other half will have the *y* allele.

These three offspring — *YY*, *Yy*, and *Yy* — represent the "3" in Mendel's 3:1 ratio. No matter how many plants he crossed, three out of every four offspring showed the dominant phenotype. One of the three had a homozygous dominant genotype; the other two were heterozygous.

The third genotype (*yy*) has two recessive alleles. No dominant alleles are present to mask the recessive allele, so these offspring all appear green. This genotype is the "1" in Mendel's 3:1 ratio.

CHAPTER three

Prediction and Probability

The word "random" means "by chance." Gregor Mendel thought alleles for a trait segregated randomly when they passed into sex cells, or gametes. If this were true, Mendel knew he could predict the results of crosses using probability. Probability is the chance, or likelihood, that a given event will occur. Probabilities are expressed as fractions, decimals, or percents. For example, in a monohybrid cross between two heterozygous parents, there is a one in four chance that any offspring will show the recessive trait. This probability is expressed as 25 percent.

Mendel knew the parents in his earliest crosses were true-breeding. But he did not know the offspring's genotypes. He did testcrosses to determine this. A testcross is a cross between an individual and its homozygous recessive parent type. For example, Mendel might cross a yellow offspring (*Yy*) from the second generation with its green (*yy*) parent type.

The offspring of such a testcross might have either a *Yy* or a *yy* genotype. Punnett squares can predict the results of crossing an individual with each genotype with one that is homozygous recessive. If

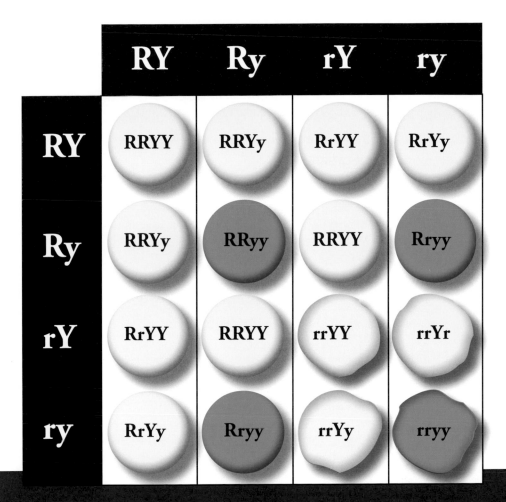

	RY	Ry	rY	ry
RY	RRYY	RRYy	RrYY	RrYy
Ry	RRYy	RRyy	RRYY	Rryy
rY	RrYY	RRYY	rrYY	rrYr
ry	RrYy	Rryy	rrYy	rryy

This Punnett square shows a dihybrid cross, in which two traits are followed together. Parents are heterozygous for both traits (genotypes RrYy) and offspring show a 9:3:3:1 ratio.

the genotype of the individual is homozygous dominant (*YY*), as shown in the left square, all offspring will have yellow phenotypes. If the genotype of the individual is heterozygous, or *Yy* (right square), half will be yellow and half will be green. By comparing the actual results of the cross with the predictions shown in the Punnett square, a researcher can determine the individual's genotype.

Mendel's testcrosses of second-generation offspring backcrossed with their green parent gave the needed information. These results showed the genotype of the second generation was heterozygous, not homozygous, because the green trait appeared. It also showed there were equal numbers of green and yellow alleles. If alleles had not sorted randomly (and equally), the seeds would not have been half yellow and half green.

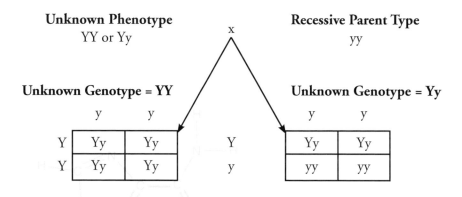

Unknown Phenotype
YY or Yy

Recessive Parent Type
yy

x

Unknown Genotype = YY

	y	y
Y	Yy	Yy
Y	Yy	Yy

Y
y

Unknown Genotype = Yy

	y	y
Y	Yy	Yy
y	yy	yy

Mendel also thought that "factors" for different traits were not connected to each other. He thought genes controlling different traits were independent and traveled separately when they entered gametes. To test this hypothesis, he conducted dihybrid crosses, using combinations of two genes.

The following Punnett square shows a dihybrid cross using two different pairs of alleles—round and wrinkled seeds, and short and tall plants. *R* indicates round (dominant) seeds and *r* indicates wrinkled (recessive) seeds. *T* represents tall (dominant) plant types and *t* represents short (recessive) plant types. Each parent donates one allele from each of the two pairs. So the possible gametes, shown outside the square, have two alleles, not one, and the offspring inside each box have two pairs of alleles.

		Alleles in Sperm			
		TR	Tr	tR	tr
	TR	TTRR	TTRr	TtRR	TtRr
Alleles in Eggs	Tr	TTRr	TTrr	TtRr	Ttrr
	tR	TtRr	TtRr	ttRR	ttRr
	tr	TtRr	Ttrr	ttRr	ttrr

A dihybrid cross has sixteen possible combinations of two gene pairs. As always, whenever a dominant allele is present, that allele appears in the phenotype. In the top row, all four genotypes have at least one dominant allele for both height and seed shape. So all four will have tall, round phenotypes. In the second row, all four have at least one dominant allele for height, but two have the *rr* genotype, which will result in a wrinkled seed shape. So of these four, two will be "tall, round" and two will be "tall, wrinkled." Combining all similar phenotypes in this way gives a set of predict-able mathematical ratios:

9/16 tall, round
3/16 tall, wrinkled
3/16 short, round
1/16 short, wrinkled

In shorthand form, this is a 9:3:3:1 ratio. Remember that a mono-hybrid cross has three different genotypes. For seed color, these were *YY*, *Yy*, and *yy*. A dihybrid cross has nine different possible genotypes. For plant height and seed shape, these were:

TTRR	TTRr	TTrr
TtRR	TtRr	Ttrr
ttRR	ttRr	ttrr

This microscope and case of slides, used by Gregor Mendel, are now part of the Mendel Museum, in the Abbey of St. Thomas, where Mendel lived.

Mendel also did trihybrid crosses, or crosses involving three traits. When he tested traits for height, seed shape, and seed color together, the same thing happened, only with more possible combinations. Three pairs of genes have twenty-seven possible genotypes.

In Mendel's dihybrid crosses, every possible combination of traits appeared in the offspring in these predictable ratios. Inheritance patterns for each trait were the same, whether they were tested separately or together. This suggested that alleles for the different traits sorted and traveled randomly. They followed the laws of probability. This confirmed Mendel's hypothesis. He developed his third law of inheritance, the law of independent assortment. It states that, during the formation of gametes, different pairs of genes undergo independent assortment. That is, they sort randomly and travel separately into the egg or sperm cell.

Mendel's Laws

1. *Theory of particulate inheritance: Discrete factors (genes) are inherited unchanged from generation to generation.*
2. *Law of segregation: Factors (genes) controlling a single trait pass separately and independently into different gametes.*
3. *Law of independent assortment: Alleles controlling different traits sort independently into different gametes.*

Often, only two of Mendel's ideas—segregation and independent assortment—are given the status of laws or principles. Particulate inheritance is not always included, but without this breakthrough, the other two laws would not have been possible.

By luck or design, Mendel chose to study exactly the right garden pea traits. He did not know about chromosomes or that many genes are located together on the same chromosome. The traits Mendel chose happened to be either on different chromosomes or far enough apart so that they sorted independently. This led him to the very neat conclusion that all traits travel separately. Later geneticists found things are not always so simple.

Does this mean that Mendel was wrong? Not at all. His laws are absolutely correct for the traits he studied and for all situations where two genes are located on different chromosomes. But other rules apply when genes for two traits are located near each other on the same chromosome.

In his eight years of studying garden pea inheritance, Gregor Mendel set the stage for the development of the entire field of genetics. His laws of inheritance formed the basis for all the research that followed. Mendel died in 1884, before people realized the importance of his contributions. Shortly before his death, he is said to have told a friend, "My time will come." And it has!

CHAPTER four

Navigating Complex Inheritance Patterns

After Gregor Mendel, geneticists began to study other traits and species. They soon realized that not all traits were inherited as neatly as Mendel's laws suggested. Not all traits were clearly dominant or recessive. Others appeared to have more than two forms, or alleles. For example, a flower had three colors instead of two. Humans had four blood types. Sometimes, a trait appeared much more frequently in men than in women. And some traits appeared to travel together. If one trait appeared in an offspring, another (often totally different) trait also appeared. These clues suggested not all inheritance followed Mendel's laws.

Incomplete Dominance

In Mendel's peas, self-crossing heterozygous purple flowers produced a 3:1 ratio of purple to white flowers in the next generation. That is, purple was completely dominant over white. But some other crosses produce a different result. When a pink snapdragon is self-crossed, half the flowers are pink. One-fourth of the offspring

Not all traits show simple inheritance patterns. The Alstroemeria flower produces several different pigments, but none is dominant. Breeders hybridize the plants to produce complex and variable color patterns.

is homozygous (*RR*) and red, one-half is heterozygous (*Rr*) and pink, and the other one-fourth is homozygous recessive (*rr*) and white.

This situation is called incomplete dominance. Both red and white alleles show some dominance, but neither completely masks the presence of the other. If Mendel had studied snapdragons instead of garden peas, he might have thought the Greek idea of blending inheritance was correct!

Codominance

In codominance, two or more alleles are expressed when present in only one "dose." Expression of the alleles is both independent

Red and white colors in this calf are codominant, but the spotted pattern is recessive. In a true roan calf, red and white hairs would be equally distributed throughout the coat.

and equal. One example is the inheritance of coat color in cattle. They have alleles for red and white coat color, named C^R and C^W. C stands for coat color. The capital letters R and W indicate that both colors are dominant. When a red bull (C^RC^R) is crossed with a white cow (C^WC^W), the resulting offspring have the genotype C^RC^W. They are all roan-colored. That is, they have a mixture of red and white hairs. The hairs are not pink, as in incomplete dominance. The animals have approximately equal numbers of red and white hairs, so they look mottled or speckled.

Multiple Alleles

The system of ABO blood types in humans illustrates both codominance and another complex inheritance pattern: multiple alleles. The human species has three different alleles that determine ABO blood types. Of course, each individual receives only two of these, one from each parent. Two of the three alleles, called I^A and I^B, are codominant. The third allele, i, is recessive. The dominant alleles cause the production of proteins, either antigen A or antigen B, on the surfaces of red blood cells. The recessive allele does not produce an antigen.

Three possible alleles combined in pairs give six possible genotypes. They can produce four different phenotypes—blood groups A, B, AB, and O. The table shows the combinations of genotypes and the phenotypes they produce.

Blood Type (Phenotype)	Possible Genotype
A	I^AI^A or I^Ai
B	I^BI^B or I^Bi
AB	I^AI^B
O	ii

Environmental Influence

Genes do not act alone to control traits. The environment always plays an important role. Melanin production in some animals is related to temperature — the points on a Siamese cat are darker than the torso because the body temperature of the ears, tail, and feet is lower. Environmental differences affect all genes. Even identical twins are unique because their environments are always slightly different.

People with type A or type B blood can be homozygous for the dominant allele. They also can be heterozygous, having one dominant and one recessive allele. People with type AB blood always have two codominant alleles. People with type O blood always have two recessive alleles.

Blood types also illustrate something important about the meaning of dominance. Sometimes, people think dominant alleles outnumber recessive alleles in a population. This is not always the case. The most common blood type in the human population is type O, with two recessive alleles. Forty-five percent of Caucasians are type O. For African Americans, the percentage is 49 percent. And for Native Americans, it is 79 percent. Dominance describes the ability to mask the recessive allele when both are present. It does not relate to numbers.

Polygenic Inheritance

Many traits in a population show continuous variation. That is, there is a range of variation, but no precise groups, such as red versus

Snowflake, an albino lowland gorilla, lived at the Barcelona Zoo until his death from skin cancer in 2003. Albinos produce no melanin, because all their pigment production genes are recessive.

white color. Human traits like hair, eye, and skin color are good examples. These continuous traits result from polygenic inheritance. They are controlled by two or more gene pairs, instead of one.

Hair, eye, and skin color result from melanin, a dark pigment. Two genes (A and B) control melanin production for skin color. Melanin production is dominant. Lack of production is recessive. A person who is homozygous recessive for both genes (aabb) produces no pigment. That person has albinism, a condition where he or she has very light skin, hair, and eyes. A person with only one dominant allele (Aabb or aaBb) is very light-skinned. A person with two dominant alleles (AAbb, AaBb, or aaBB) has medium skin color. A person with three dominant alleles (AABb or AaBB) has very dark skin, and one with all dominant alleles (AABB) has completely black skin.

A similar situation exists for hair and eye color. Melanin colors the iris of the eye. The more melanin produced, the darker the eye color. One main gene controls eye color. Dominant allele B controls production of brown, green, hazel, or gray eyes. Recessive allele b controls production of blue eyes. A blue-eyed person has very little melanin. But several other genes control the amount and distribution of melanin, so there is a continuous range of eye colors, as there is a continuous range of skin colors.

CHAPTER five

Mitosis: The Cellular Copy Machine

There are two kinds of nuclear reproduction. The first kind, mitosis, makes exact copies of a nucleus. Mitosis (followed by the division of the rest of the cell) keeps the number of body cells constant. It replaces dead and injured cells. Mitosis is also how a body grows. Every person starts out life as a fertilized egg, or zygote. An adult human body contains about seventy-five to one hundred trillion cells, all of which came from that original zygote. All were made by mitosis.

Linking Genetics and Cell Reproduction

Mendel showed that traits were passed from generation to generation. His laws explain how he thought this happened. But Mendel had no direct evidence because he did not know what went on inside the cells of his peas. The explanation came with the discovery of chromosomes during the late nineteenth and early twentieth centuries.

People thought genetic information was contained in the cell nucleus. But they didn't know the nature of that information or how it was transferred. Walther Flemming, a German anatomist, used a

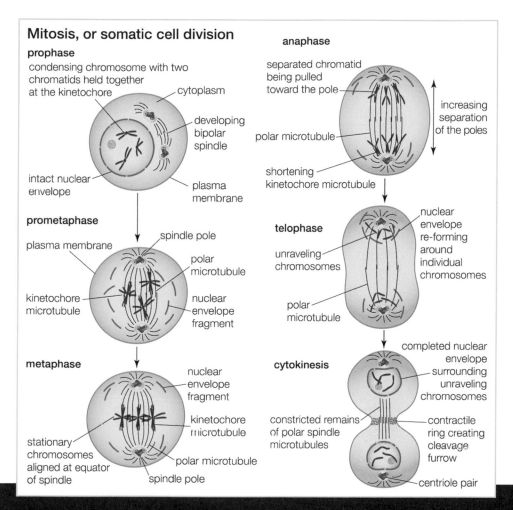

Mitosis, or somatic cell division

prophase
condensing chromosome with two chromatids held together at the kinetochore
cytoplasm
developing bipolar spindle
intact nuclear envelope
plasma membrane

prometaphase
plasma membrane
spindle pole
polar microtubule
kinetochore microtubule
nuclear envelope fragment

metaphase
nuclear envelope fragment
kinetochore microtubule
stationary chromosomes aligned at equator of spindle
polar microtubule
spindle pole

anaphase
separated chromatid being pulled toward the pole
increasing separation of the poles
polar microtubule
shortening kinetochore microtubule

telophase
unraveling chromosomes
polar microtubule
nuclear envelope re-forming around individual chromosomes

cytokinesis
constricted remains of polar spindle microtubules
completed nuclear envelope surrounding unraveling chromosomes
contractile ring creating cleavage furrow
centriole pair

These mitosis diagrams show how duplicated cells line up and separate their chromosomes. The two daughter cells formed during cytokinesis are identical to each other and to the mother cell.

microscope to investigate cell nuclei. Flemming stained the cells with dyes. This produced a very dark network of fibers inside the nucleus. Flemming called it chromatin. He saw that during nuclear division (mitosis), the network became a series of threadlike bodies. These were eventually named chromosomes.

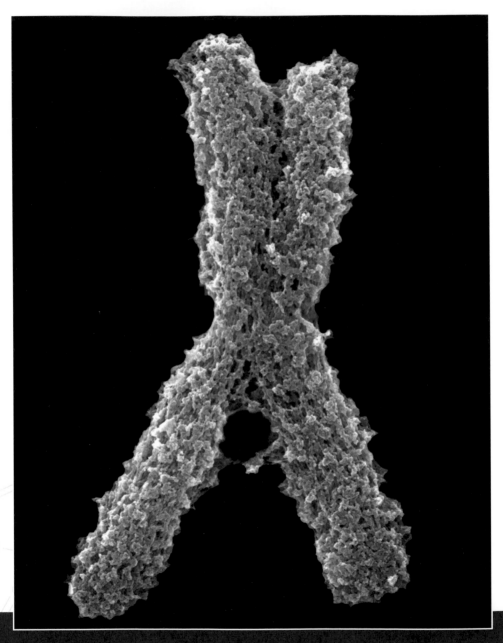

This scanning electron micrograph shows a single chromosome, or DNA molecule. The presence of two chromatids indicates that DNA has duplicated. Color has been artificially added.

DNA, Chromosomes, and Genes

Mitosis transfers genetic information from cell to cell. It begins with the genetic material, or DNA molecule. "DNA" is short for "deoxyribonucleic acid." Most DNA in higher organisms resides in the cell nucleus. The DNA of each chromosome is divided into genes. Each gene controls or helps control a single trait. Together, all the genes control all the traits that make up the body's structures and functions. These include everything from eye color to hormone production.

Each organism has a specific number of chromosomes. Humans have forty-six chromosomes in twenty-three pairs. Mendel's garden peas have fourteen chromosomes in seven pairs. This is the diploid, or *2n* number, of chromosomes.

If a cell is going to divide, it grows to a certain size. Then it duplicates its DNA. The two DNA copies separate, and the cell divides to form two new cells. Each new cell now has one complete copy of the DNA. So the two new cells, called daughter cells, are identical to the original (mother) cell. This sequence may be repeated, becoming a cell cycle.

The Phases of Mitosis

The cell cycle is divided into steps, or phases. The phases are a bit hard to define because the cycle is a continuous process. But you can identify each phase in a microscope slide of dividing cells, such as an onion root tip. The cell spends up to 90 percent of its time in interphase, before mitosis begins. Individual chromosomes cannot be seen during this time. They appear as the darkly stained network described by Flemming. During interphase, the cell increases in size and its DNA replicates.

When the cell contains two copies of all its DNA, it's ready for mitosis. The first stage is prophase. DNA molecules shorten and coil

Cancer: When Mitosis Loses Control

Cell division in the body is normally under exquisite control. But sometimes, mitosis goes wild. A glitch, or mutation, causes the cell cycle to break down. The cell becomes a cancer cell. It divides without control and forms a lumpy mass of cells called a tumor.

Cancers vary, but all cancer cells show abnormal, disorganized growth. They crowd out healthy cells and prevent them from doing their jobs. Cancer cells cannot carry out the functions of normal cells. They break apart, move to other locations, and form new tumors—a process called metastasis. Cancer cells may cause death if untreated. Because the cells are unable to control their own growth, doctors must kill the cells through surgery, drugs, or other treatments.

into compact, visible chromosomes. They are spread randomly through the cell. They are double structures with two parts, or chromatids, held together by a centromere. Each chromatid contains one copy of the DNA. During prophase, the nuclear membrane begins to disappear and two structures called centrosomes migrate to opposite sides of the cell.

Then comes metaphase. The centromeres of all the chromosomes line up in single file down the center, or "equator" region of the cell. The chromatids hang over each side of the centerline. Each chromosome moves independently, so they can line up in any order. Members of a pair are not necessarily near each other in line. Spindle fibers stretch between each centromere and the two centrioles, which are located at opposite poles of the cell.

During anaphase, centromeres break apart and separate the chromatids. They travel to opposite sides of the cell. As soon as they separate, the chromatids are called chromosomes. In animal cells, the spindle fibers, which are attached to each centromere, pull them away from the middle of the cell. In telophase, the two sets of DNA have completely separated from each other. A new nuclear membrane forms around each set. The chromosomes relax and return to their interphase state. Near the end of telophase, the whole cell divides. A new cell membrane forms around each set of DNA. This cell-separation process is called cytokinesis.

As a result of mitosis and cytokinesis, one cell becomes two. Each new cell has one complete copy of the body's DNA, containing all the genes. The cell still has the diploid number of chromosomes—forty-six in humans. The two new, genetically identical cells, now in interphase, will grow in size. Soon they will duplicate their DNA, and each may continue its own cell cycle.

This nerve has been harvested from a boy's right arm. Along with nerves taken from his mother, it will be transplanted into his left arm to help repair an injury.

How Fast Do Cells Divide?

How fast cells reproduce depends on the type of cell. In very active cells, such as skin cells, the whole cycle takes about twenty-four hours. Mitosis itself lasts only about an hour. Under normal conditions, the entire epidermis, or outer layer of skin cells, replaces itself by mitosis every fifty-two to seventy-five days. When an injury occurs, mitosis speeds up to quickly replace the damaged cells.

Other cell types replace themselves very slowly. Until recently, scientists thought nerve cells could never be replaced. They thought each person was born with all of his or her nerve cells, and the brain slowly degenerated over a lifetime. But now we know that some nerve cells can slowly replace themselves. If scientists can "turn on" young nerve cells, or stimulate them to reproduce, these new cells can replace missing or damaged cells. Eventually, this could help treat diseases, such as multiple sclerosis and Parkinson's disease, and it could help repair brain and spinal cord injuries.

CHAPTER six

From Parent to Child:
The Story of Variation

Mitosis makes exact copies of cell nuclei within an organism. The second kind of nuclear reproduction is meiosis. It makes sex cells, or gametes, which pass from one generation to the next. Sexual reproduction begins with gamete production. Gametes are made in the body's sex organs—ovaries in women and testes in men. Sexual reproduction is the major cause of variation. It is the reason why no two organisms are alike.

A few years after Walther Flemming's work on mitosis, another German, Theodor Boveri, studied chromosomes in gametes. He studied *Ascaris*, a parasitic roundworm with only two pairs of chromosomes. Boveri saw that, during gamete formation, the chromosome number decreased from four to two. The number returned to four after fertilization. This was one of the first descriptions of meiosis.

At the turn of the twentieth century, American Walter Sutton studied meiosis in the lubber grasshopper. He identified its eleven pairs of chromosomes, plus a single sex chromosome. He described the stages of meiosis, following the progress of each chromosome.

Meiosis, or sex cell division

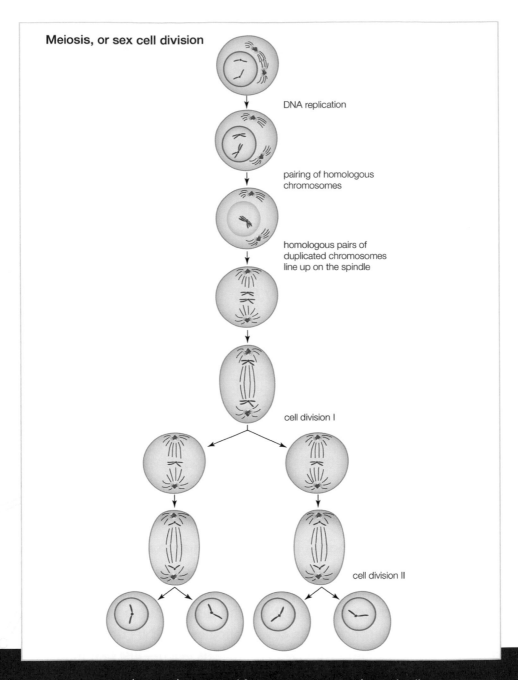

DNA replication

pairing of homologous chromosomes

homologous pairs of duplicated chromosomes line up on the spindle

cell division I

cell division II

Meiosis I causes reduction division and forms two new, nonidentical cells. In Meiosis II, division proceeds exactly as in mitosis. Each cell produces two cells, each identical to their mother cell.

as in mitosis. The chromosomes are randomly mixed, and the centrioles begin to migrate to opposite poles of the cell.

But Metaphase I is different from mitosis. During meiosis, chromosomes do not line up in single file down the center of the cell. Instead of forty-six individuals, they become twenty-three pairs. Members of homologous pairs find each other and line up side-by-side, one on either side of the cell's centerline. Spindle fibers stretch from each centromere to the centrioles at the two poles. So, at the end of metaphase, the chromosomes are neatly arranged in pairs, rather than lined up single file.

Often, when homologous chromosomes pair during metaphase, a special process called crossing-over occurs. The two inside chromatids "tangle" and end up exchanging pieces. This changes the arrangement of alleles on the homologous chromosomes. Some of the original mother's genes are now on the original father's chromosome, and vice versa. When the chromosomes separate, each gamete has a new combination of alleles. Crossing-over is one way meiosis creates variation in gametes.

During anaphase of Meiosis I, the paired chromosomes—some now with different gene combinations—move apart and go toward opposite sides of the cell. This is the second way variation occurs during meiosis. Homologous pairs have separated forever.

In Telophase I, nuclear membranes form around the two new sets of chromosomes. Chromosomes return to their relaxed interphase state. Cytokinesis occurs. At the end of Meiosis I, there are two new cells. Each cell has a reduced chromosome number—half the number in the original cell. This is the haploid, or n, number. Each gamete will give only half the parent's genes to an offspring.

Meiosis II and Gametogenesis

Both new cells now carry out a second division, Meiosis II. This time, the nuclear material divides by exactly the same process as mitosis.

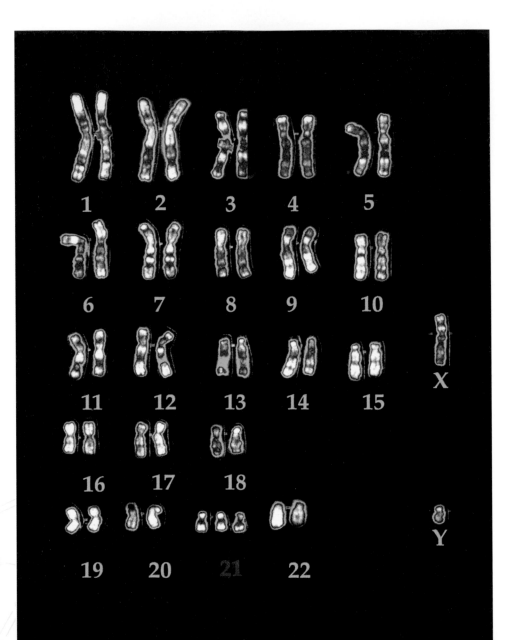

The condition shown here is trisomy 21 (an extra chromosome 21), which results in Down syndrome. The karyotype has an XY chromosome pair, so this person is male.

Each new cell gets one chromosome (consisting of a single chromatid with one copy of the DNA) for each homologous pair in the original cell. Meiosis II begins with two cells, so the end result is four cells. Because of reduction division and crossing-over in Meiosis I, all are different from the original starting cell.

Gametogenesis, or gamete formation, is not complete when chromosomes separate. In human males, cytokinesis during Meiosis II results in equal division of the cytoplasm. It ends with four cells of the same size. These four cells begin to change shape. Most of the cytoplasm forms into a long tail. Gametogenesis in males makes four tiny but functional sperm cells. All the father's genetic material is preserved. Not all of it will be used because only one sperm can fertilize an egg. Nevertheless, it is all available.

In females, nuclear division happens exactly the same as in males. But the division of cytoplasm is unequal. One daughter cell in Meiosis I receives most of the cytoplasm, so it is bigger than the other. The same thing happens during Meiosis II. The largest cell becomes an egg cell. The other three cells, called polar bodies, die. So any mother cell only forms one functional egg cell. One-half the mother's genetic information is lost.

Fertilization: The Final Journey

Genes are thoroughly mixed during meiosis. Crossing-over occurs in Metaphase I. Paired chromosomes separate randomly in Anaphase I. Genetic information is lost when an egg is formed. So the eggs and sperm produced are considerably different from the parent's starting cell. Meiosis and gametogenesis have produced variation.

Fertilization causes more variation. Because of reduction division, human egg and sperm cells have only twenty-three chromosomes each—one member of each pair, randomly selected from the original pair. From millions of sperm cells produced, only one will fertilize the egg cell. The genetic mix of this one lucky sperm cell will be entirely

Meiosis and Nondisjunction

Like mitosis, meiosis can go wrong. Sometimes, when chromosome pairs line up during Meiosis I, members of a chromosome pair stick together. Two chromosomes will go into the same cell, and none will go into the other cell in that division. The resulting gametes will either have an extra chromosome, or they will lack one. Failure of chromosomes to separate correctly during meiosis is called nondisjunction. It results in specific genetic disorders.

Every chromosome contains many genes, so an extra or missing chromosome affects the entire body. An extra copy of chromosome 21 causes trisomy 21, or Down syndrome. People with Down syndrome often have a number of easily recognized physical traits. These include short stature and weak muscles, as well as facial features such as small, low-set ears and abnormal shapes of the mouth, palate, and tongue. These children may also have cognitive disabilities and heart defects.

random. In humans, only one egg cell per month will mature and be available for fertilization. Again, the genetic mix in the egg cell will be random. When the single set of genes in the egg combines with the single set in the sperm, the third and final form of variation occurs. The mother's and the father's genes will mix and form an entirely new combination of genes. The result will be a unique individual.

CHAPTER seven

Gene Linkage: Riding the Chromosome Train

Linked genes travel together during meiosis. They do not follow Mendel's third law and undergo independent assortment. Linkage occurs because chromosomes, not genes, separate during meiosis. When gametes are formed, each separated chromosome passes into a particular gamete. All the genes on that chromosome go along for the ride, like cars on the same train. So dihybrid crosses involving linked traits do not show the same 9:3:3:1 ratios found in traits that assort separately.

In fact, linkage has exactly the opposite effect of meiosis and fertilization. Linkage decreases variation, while these processes increase it. When a cross produces more parental-type offspring than predicted by independent assortment, this is a clue that linkage is occurring.

The simplest way to define linkage groups, or genes that travel together, is by the number of chromosome pairs in the cells of an organism. Humans have twenty-three pairs of chromosomes and twenty-three linkage groups. Mendel's peas have seven pairs of chromosomes and seven linkage groups. But linkage is not this simple. Because of crossing-over, genes located on the same chromosome

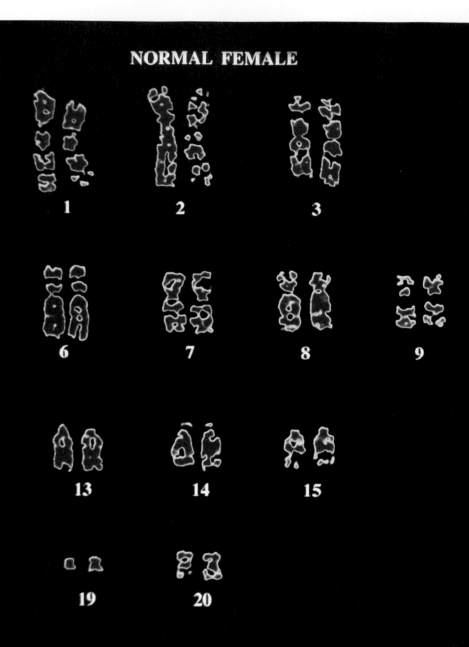

NORMAL FEMALE

1 2 3

6 7 8 9

13 14 15

19 20

This karyotype shows a normal female with two X chromosomes. One X in each pair (the "Barr body") is inactive, so both sexes have only one active copy of the X chromosome.

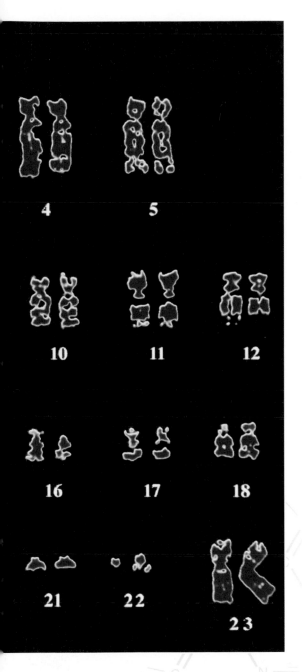

4   5

10   11   12

16   17   18

21   22

23

can still behave as though they are not linked.

Genes and DNA Structure

To understand how linkage happens, it helps to understand something about the structure of DNA and chromosomes. A chromosome consists of a very long molecule of DNA associated with numerous protein molecules. This DNA molecule is made of tiny repeating units called nucleotides. Each nucleotide contains an even tinier unit called a base. There are only four types of bases in the DNA molecule. The DNA molecule consists of two strands, and the bases connect in specific pairs to hook the strands together.

The order, or sequence, of base pairs along the strand defines different genes. Genes vary greatly in length, but an average gene is about five thousand base pairs (bp) long. Each gene contains a code determined by the sequences of bases along its length. This genetic code tells the cell how to make a certain protein. Together, the

Thomas Hunt Morgan (1866–1945) and his students extended Mendel's results by unraveling gene linkage in the fruit fly. Morgan also proposed that variation could occur by crossing-over.

body's proteins determine the structures, functions, and behaviors that make each person unique. As you have seen, environmental factors affect how traits are expressed. Also, most traits result from more than one gene. But every protein must be made correctly and in a precise amount for the trait to be expressed.

People have about 20,500 identified genes scattered along their chromosomes. Each gene helps make as many as six different proteins. Between the genes are long, repeating segments of noncoding (non-gene) DNA, often misleadingly referred to as "junk DNA." Altogether, humans' forty-six chromosomes have almost three billion base pairs. Probably only about 5 percent of these are actually part of a gene.

When Are Genes Linked?

The distance between any two genes is measured in numbers of base pairs. This distance determines how likely two genes are to be linked. In general, if two genes on a chromosome are closer than fifty million bp, they will be linked. That is, they are more than 50 percent likely to travel together when chromosomes separate during meiosis. They follow Mendel's law of independent assortment. But if they are farther apart than fifty million base pairs, there is an increased chance they will not travel together. This is because of crossing-over.

The specific location of a gene along a chromosome is called its locus. If two gene loci are close together, crossing-over will probably not occur. But the farther apart the two loci are, the more likely it is that breaks and crossing-over will occur. If two genes are far enough apart, they act like they are on different chromosomes.

Discovering Linkage: Morgan's Fruit Flies

American geneticist Thomas Hunt Morgan won a Nobel Prize for dis-covering and describing patterns of gene linkage. Morgan and his

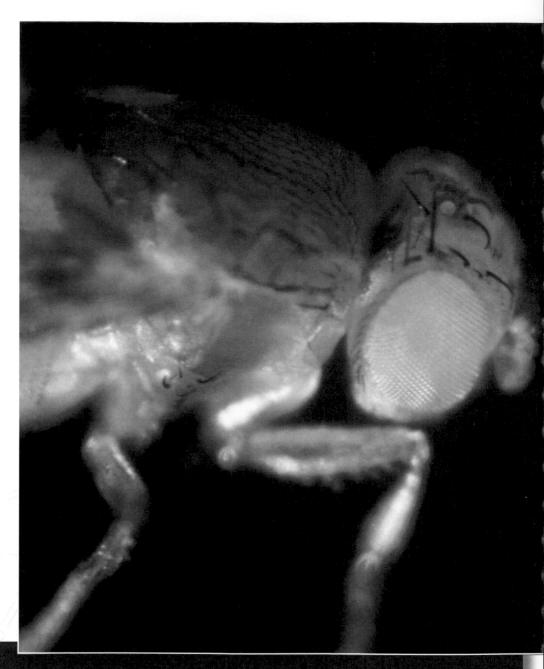

Thomas Hunt Morgan studied the normal ("wild type") red-eyed fruit fly (right) and a white-eyed mutation (left). Crosses of these and other fly mutations helped him explain gene linkage.

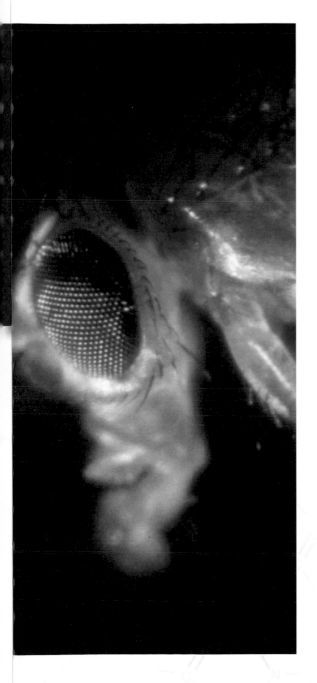

students knew that certain fruit flies have four pairs of chromosomes, including one pair of sex chromosomes. As in humans, females have two large X chromosomes and males have one X and one much smaller Y chromosome. However, unlike the situation in humans, the fruit fly's Y chromosome does not determine its maleness—it is male if only one X chromosome is present and female if there are two. With only one X chromosome, there was never a dominant chromosome to mask the recessive allele.

Over several decades, Morgan and his students discovered forty different fruit fly mutations. They bred large numbers of each mutant type. Then, just like Mendel, they did testcrosses to determine patterns of inheritance.

Testcrosses with the white-eyed mutation led Morgan to question Mendel's laws. When he crossed red-eyed females with white-eyed males, first- and second-generation offspring both followed Mendel's laws. First-generation flies were all red-eyed and the second generation

CHAPTER eight

Gene Mapping and Beyond

Throughout the mid-twentieth century, scientists worked out the structure of the DNA molecule. In 1953, American James Watson and Englishman Francis Crick described DNA as a double helix. In 1966, the "genetic code" was cracked when research showed that each group of three bases along a gene coded for an amino acid. Pulling amino acids together in the same sequence as DNA's base triplets made a protein. This proved that DNA's function was to make proteins.

These discoveries meant geneticists no longer had to study genes indirectly by looking at phenotypes. In 1972, American Paul Berg made the first artificial recombinant DNA molecule by splicing DNA from one species of bacteria into another species. Now scientists could not only study actual genes, they could also manipulate and clone them. Genetic engineering had begun.

The Promise of Modern Genetics

Geneticists quickly realized the implications of DNA research. One was the promise of new and better foods and drugs. A gene from

James Watson (right) and Francis Crick show their "double helix" model of DNA. Scientists Maurice Wilkins and Rosalind Franklin also helped explain DNA structure.

another organism can now be spliced into a crop plant to make it more nutritious or disease-resistant. A cow can be engineered to produce more milk. Foreign genes are inserted into bacteria so that they can produce drug products such as human insulin and human growth hormone.

Another promise of genetics is the ability to treat genetic disorders. This requires analyzing genomes. A genome is the complete set of all genes in all chromosomes of an organism. Understanding the genome of any organism requires long, painstaking work. It can be divided into two parts: gene sequencing and gene mapping.

Base Sequences

A base sequence is a complete list of bases found in all genes on all chromosomes of an organism, in order. The four bases can be abbreviated A, T, C, and G. A base sequence is a long list of these four letters with no spaces. They are not neatly divided into "words" or "sentences," so just looking at the sequence won't tell you what it means.

Base sequences are always huge. The bacterium *E. coli* contains a mere 4,600,000 base pairs. Assuming 3,000 characters per page, it would take 1,533 pages to print it all. Thomas Hunt Morgan's tiny fruit fly contains 180,000,000 bases—that's 60,000 pages. Most people would think the human genome, with 3 billion base pairs, has the most bases and genes. However, a grasshopper has 180 billion base pairs, and a single-celled amoeba has about 670 billion.

Many of the nongene, or "junk," sequences in a genome are repeated over and over. Organisms with the largest genomes seem to have the most junk DNA. Until recently, people thought it had no function. But now they realize that some of it has a variety of cell functions, including regulating aspects of protein synthesis.

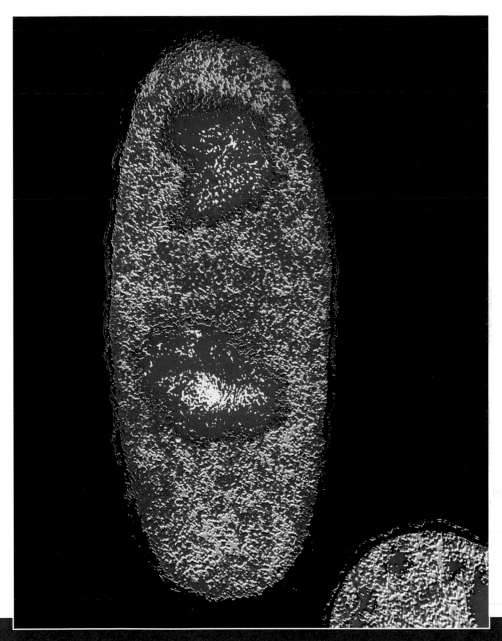

False-color transmission electron micrograph of a section through the bacterium E. coli. *The DNA appears as pale fibrils within the two blue patches.* E. coli *contains 4,600,000 base pairs.*

The Human Genome Project

Scientists quickly began to work out base sequences of important research organisms. These included *E. coli*, yeast, and the fruit fly. As they analyzed DNA, it became clear that many genes are almost identical in all organisms. Closely related organisms have more DNA in common. Half of fruit fly DNA is identical to human DNA. Humans and mice have 85 percent of their DNA in common, and humans and chimpanzees have 98 percent. Not surprisingly, some identical genes act the same. Genes for smell or taste act the same in nematode worms as they do in humans. Studying immunity genes in chickens helps us understand human immunity.

Sequencing the human genome was the purpose of the Human Genome Project, first proposed in 1985. Many people considered this project impossible. Others compared it to landing a man on the Moon. But in 1987, the first automated DNA sequencing machine became commercially available. Scientists began the Human Genome Project in 1990, and in 2000, a rough draft of the human genome was published. A much improved and corrected version followed in 2003. The human genome still has gaps, but scientists in laboratories all over the world continue to work on this massive project.

By 2009, 1,069 species, most of them bacteria, had been completely sequenced. Many are disease-causing bacteria and fungi. Others include honeybees, mice, rats, dogs, rice, poplar trees, cows, chimpanzees, mosquitoes, and puffer fish.

Gene Mapping

Gene maps, as well as base sequences, are needed to understand genomes. A gene map is similar to a city map. It locates every gene precisely by placing it at the correct locus on the correct chromosome. One author compared locating a specific gene to locating

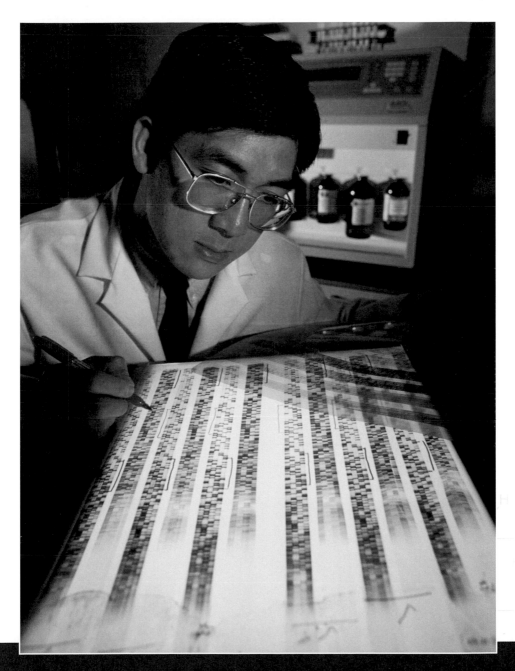

In DNA sequencing, long sequences of nucleotides are scanned to find regions of identical DNA. This locates genes on a chromosome and can help narrow down their functions.

a person in New York City given a picture but no name, address, or telephone number.

Like Alfred Sturtevant's first map of the fruit fly's X chromosome, gene maps are still basically straight lines with "markers," or locations of known genes or DNA sequences, identified along their lengths. Some are physical maps, showing the exact number of base pairs between markers. Others are gene-linkage maps, such as Sturtevant's. They show gene locations in relation to each other, relative distances between genes, and likely linkage patterns. Sturtevant had only

Tracking a Gene

To track the precise gene causing a genetic defect, scientists follow two basic steps:

I. Find the protein causing the defect.

    A. Study disorder phenotypes (traits) using family histories and pedigrees.
    B. Compare karyotypes (chromosome pictures) to find abnormal chromosomes.
    C. Study proteins in affected individuals to locate those with defects.
    D. Find structure of affected proteins (determine their amino acid sequence).

II. Use the protein to locate the gene.

    A. Work backward from the protein's amino acid sequence to find its DNA sequence.
    B. Search (screen) a "DNA library" (database of known DNA sequences) to find DNA segments used in the specific cells or tissues affected by the genetic defect. This is a complex, multistep process.

phenotypes to determine gene locations. Geneticists can now locate unique, nonrepeating DNA sequences, which are most likely genes.

The Future of Genetics

About 92.3 percent of the human gene sequence is now complete, although additions and corrections are still being made. Each segment in the DNA "library" must be identified as either part of a gene coding for a protein or a segment of junk DNA. Each new gene locus that is pinpointed is a marker that makes it easier to find more new genes.

Geneticists are still not sure of the importance of the long strands of junk DNA. But they have discovered that some of these repeating

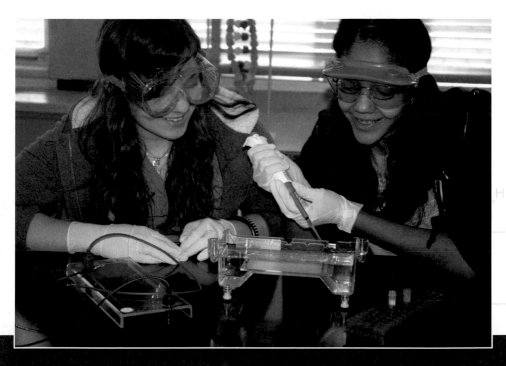

High school students carry out gel electrophoresis to determine relative sizes of DNA fragments. An electrical current separates fragments by size as they travel through a gel.

segments can be used to identify individuals. This is the basis of DNA fingerprinting, which is now used—among other things—to determine family relationships and identify criminal suspects.

Continuing research into the human genome—and genomes of many other organisms—will likely transform our future. Among other things, geneticists will use this information to map locations of genes causing specific disorders and develop treatments. They are tracing the history and evolution of life on Earth. They hope to increase understanding of how the body works, how we are related to other organisms, and how we can use genetics to benefit our culture and environment.

In short, we have traveled light-years in understanding genetics since Gregor Mendel's time, but we still have far to go. Analyzing the human genome has barely begun. And determining how to use the wealth of information contained in it will be the work of many generations.

Glossary

allele An alternative form of a gene, such as blue or brown eye color, or round or wrinkled seeds.

chromosome Structure in the cell nucleus composed of a single DNA molecule and containing many genes along its length.

dihybrid cross A genetic cross in which two traits (genes) are followed and the phenotypes counted.

diploid Having two sets of chromosomes, one set from each parent; this occurs in all body cells. The diploid number of human chromosomes ($2n$) is forty-six, or twenty-three pairs.

dominant Condition in which one allele masks the presence of another (recessive) allele of the same gene.

gamete Sex cell (egg, or ovum, in females and sperm in males); each gamete has only one member of each pair of chromosomes and therefore only half the organism's genetic information.

gene The unit or factor that determines a trait; located in a DNA molecule (chromosome) inside every cell nucleus; for example, the gene for eye color.

genome The complete set of all genes in all chromosomes of an organism.

genotype The pair of alleles that combine in an organism to produce a phenotype; for example, *BB* or *Bb* for brown eye color and bb for blue eye color.

haploid Having one set of chromosomes; occurs in gametes as a result of meiosis (reduction division). The haploid number of human chromosomes (n) is twenty-three.

heterozygous Having two different alleles in the genotype; for example, *Yy*.

homologous chromosome Member of a pair of chromosomes in a diploid organism; homologous chromosome pairs are identical in size, shape, and sequence of genes.

homozygous Having two identical alleles in the genotype; for example, *YY* or *yy*.

hybrid An offspring produced by crossing two genetically different parents of different types; combines traits of both parents.

meiosis The nuclear division process used to form gametes; includes a reduction division, which halves the chromosome number and increases variation in offspring.

mitosis The nuclear division process used in the growth, maintenance, and repair of organisms; results in production of two identical daughter cells from a single parent cell.

monohybrid cross A genetic cross in which only one trait (gene) is followed and the phenotypes counted.

mutation Alteration in the genetic makeup (DNA sequence) of an organism; affects the genotype and often the phenotype.

natural selection The primary process by which evolution occurs; results when certain genetic types in a population are more successful than others in contributing offspring to the next generation.

phenotype The visible traits of an organism, such as eye color, seed color, or seed type.

probability The chance, or likelihood, that a given event will occur; can be expressed as a fraction, decimal, or percentage (for example, ¼, 0.25, or 25 percent).

Punnett square Diagram illustrating the results of a cross by showing all possible combinations of genotype.

recessive Condition in which the expression of one allele is masked by the presence of another (dominant) allele of the same gene.

selective breeding Artificially influencing the inheritance of traits by selecting the parents of each new generation.

testcross A cross between an individual displaying the dominant phenotype and a homozygous recessive individual; used to determine an individual's genotype.

For More Information

Canadian Association of Genetic Counsellors
P.O. Box 52083
Oakville, ON L6J 7N5
Canada
(905) 847-1363
Web site: http://www.cagc-accg.ca
This organization for professional genetic counselors and students seeks
to increase understanding and awareness of the field. The Web site
includes information on the purposes of genetic counseling and links to
related sites.

Genome Canada
150 Metcalfe Street
Ottawa, ON K2P 1P1
Canada
(613) 751-4460
Web site: http://genomecanada.ca/en
Genome Canada is a nonprofit organization dedicated to advancing
genome research for the benefit of all Canadians. The Web site
includes a section titled "Information for the Public" that gives basic
information relating genomics to agriculture, environment, forestry,
and fisheries, as well as human health.

National Human Genome Research Institute (NHGRI)
Communications and Public Liaison Branch
National Institutes of Health
Building 31, Room 4B09
31 Center Drive, MSC 2152
9000 Rockville Pike

Bethesda, MD 20892-2152

(301) 402-0911

Web site: http://www.genome.gov

The NHGRI led the project to sequence the human genome and is now leading the research to understand its structure, function, and role in health and disease. The site has an "Educational Resources" section with information on the Human Genome Project, plus basic genetics information.

National Newborn Screening and Genetics Resource Center (NNSGRC)

1912 W. Anderson Lane, Suite 210

Austin, TX 78757

(512) 454-6419

Web site: http://genes-r-us.uthscsa.edu/index.htm

The NNSGRC provides general information and resources for health professionals, communities and governments, and the general public. It discusses types of genetic conditions that are evaluated with newborn screening and gives information on each condition.

Positive Exposure

43 East 20th Street

New York, NY 10003

(212) 420-1931

Web site: http://www.positiveexposure.org/about.html

This arts organization was founded by a former fashion photographer and an M.D./Ph.D. to work with individuals and families living with genetic differences. Its gives workshops, educational and human-rights programs, and multimedia exhibitions to educate physicians, health care workers, schools, and the public about genetic differences.

U.S. Department of Energy

1000 Independence Avenue SW

Washington, DC 20585

Web site: http://genomics.energy.gov

The U.S. Department of Energy is one of the founders of the Human Genome Project and runs many genetics projects, including a Microbial Genome Program, that focus on the sequencing of microbes important in research, ecology, and energy systems. The site is filled with images and educational materials.

Web Sites

Due to the changing nature of Internet links, Rosen Publishing has developed an online list of Web sites related to the subject of this book. This site is updated regularly. Please use this link to access the list:

http://www.rosenlinks.com/gen/intro

For Further Reading

Levitin, Sonia. *The Goodness Gene*. New York, NY: Dutton Juvenile, 2005.

Mawer, Simon. *Gregor Mendel: Planting the Seeds of Genetics*. New York, NY: Harry N. Abrams, 2006.

Morgan, Sally. *From Mendel's Peas to Genetic Fingerprinting: Discovering Inheritance* (Chain Reactions). Mankato, MN: Heinemann-Raintree, 2006.

Pasachoff, Naomi E. *Barbara McClintock: Genius of Genetics*. Berkeley Heights, NJ: Enslow Publishers, 2006.

Patterson, James. *The Angel Experiment*. New York, NY: Little, Brown Young Readers, 2005.

Pobst, Sandra. *National Geographic Investigates: Animals on the Edge: Science Races to Save Species Threatened with Extinction*. Des Moines, IA: National Geographic Children's Books, 2008.

Sandvold, Lynnette Brent. *Genetics*. Tarrytown, NY: Marshall Cavendish, 2009.

Schultz, Mark. *The Stuff of Life: A Graphic Guide to Genetics and DNA*. New York, NY: Hill and Wang, 2009.

Simpson, Kathleen. *National Geographic Investigates: Genetics: From DNA to Designer Dogs*. Des Moines, IA: National Geographic Children's Books, 2008.

Werlin, Nancy. *Double Helix*. London, England: Puffin, 2005.

Bibliography

Avers, Charlotte J. *Genetics*. New York, NY: D. Van Nostrand and Company, 1980.

Children's Health. "Down Syndrome—Symptoms." WebMD, 1995–2008. Retrieved August 13, 2009 (http://children.webmd.com/tc/down-syndrome-symptoms).

Field Museum. "Gregor Mendel: Planting the Seeds of Genetics." Retrieved June 9, 2009 (http://www.fieldmuseum.org/mendel/story_heredity.asp).

Genetics Encyclopedia. *Genetics*. Farmington Hills, MI: The Gale Group, Inc., 2003.

Genomes Online. "Complete Published Genome Projects: 1069." 2009. Retrieved August 13, 2009 (http://www.genomesonline.org/gold.cgi?want=Published+Complete+Genomes).

Greenwood, Tracey, and Richard Allen. *Senior Biology 1: Student Resource and Activity Manual*. Hamilton, NZ: Biozone International, Ltd., 2004.

Hales, Karen G. "Timeline of the History of Genetics," Department of Biology, Davidson College, Davidson, NC, 2007. Retrieved August 15, 2009 (http://www.bio.davidson.edu/people/kahales/301Genetics/timeline.html#top).

Hoath, Steven B., and D. G. Leahy. "The Organization of Human Epidermis: Functional Epidermal Units and Phi Proportionality." *Journal of Investigative Dermatology* 121: 1,440–1,446, December 2003. Retrieved August 13, 2009 (http://www.nature.com/jid/journal/v121/n6/full/5602084a.html#Epidermal-replacement-rates).

Kandel, Eric R. "Thomas Hunt Morgan at Columbia University: Genes, Chromosomes, and the Origins of Modern Biology." Retrieved August 1, 2009 (http://www.columbia.edu/cu/alumni/Magazine/Morgan/morgan.html).

Lewis, Ricki. *Human Genetics: Concepts and Applications*. 8th ed. New York, NY: McGraw-Hill Higher Education, 2008.

Lindvall, Ollie, and Ron McKay. "Brain Repair by Cell Replacement and Regeneration." *National Academy of Sciences* 100 (13): 7,430–7,431,

2003. Retrieved August 13, 2009 (http://www.pnas.org/content/100/13/7430.full).

National Center for Biotechnology Information. Various data. U.S. National Library of Medicine, Bethesda, MD, 2009. Retrieved August 15, 2009 (http://www.ncbi.nlm.nih.gov).

O'Connor, Clare, and Ilona Miko. "Gene Inheritance and Transmission." 2008. Retrieved August 1, 2009 (Adapted from "Developing the Chromosome Theory," *Nature Education* 1(1) and http://www.nature.com/scitable/topicpage/Developing-the-Chromosome-Theory-164).

O'Neil, Dennis. "Mendel's Genetics." 1997–2009. Retrieved June 5, 2009 (http://anthro.palomar.edu/mendel/mendel_1.htm).

Robinson, Tara Rodden. *Genetics for Dummies.* 1st ed. Hoboken, NJ: Wiley Publishing, Inc., 2005.

Ruder, Kate, and Edward R. Winstead. "A Quick Guide to Sequenced Genomes." Genome News Network, J. Craig Venter Institute, 2004. Retrieved August 15, 2009 (http://www.genomenewsnetwork.org/resources/sequenced_genomes/genome_guide_p1.shtml).

ScienceDaily. "Human Gene Count Tumbles Again." January 15, 2008. Retrieved August 15, 2009 (http://www.sciencedaily.com/releases/2008/01/080113161406.htm).

Shaw, Kenna R. Mills, Katie Van Horne, Hubert Zhang, and Joann Boughman. "Essay Contest Reveals Misconceptions of High School Students in Genetics Content." *Genetics*, 178(3): 1157—1168, March 2008. Retrieved August 1, 2009 (http://www.pubmedcentral.nih.gov/articlerender.fcgi?artid=2278104).

Starr, Cecie, and Ralph Taggart. *Cell Biology and Genetics.* Florence, KY: Thomson Brooks/Cole, 2006.

Welsh, Michael J., and Alan E. Smith. "Cystic Fibrosis." *Scientific American*, vol. 273, 1995, pp. 53–59.

Willett, Edward. *Genetics Demystified.* 1st ed. New York, NY: McGraw-Hill Professional, 2005.

Index

About the Author

Carol Hand has a Ph.D. in zoology. For the past eleven years, she has written middle and high school science curricula for a nationally known education company. She has also taught college biology and written for standardized testing companies, and she writes nonfiction books for children and teens.

Photo Credits

Cover (top) © www.istockphoto.com/ChristianAnthony; cover (bottom), back cover, and interior © www.istockphoto.com/Gregory Spencer; p. 5 © www.istockphoto.com/Michelle Malven; p. 7 Kay Churnush/Riser/Getty Images; p. 9 Hulton Archive/Getty Images; pp. 13, 26 © James King-Holmes/Photo Researchers, Inc.; p. 14 © Sheila Terry/Photo Researchers, Inc.; p. 17 © Laguna Design/ Photo Researchers, Inc.; p. 19 © SPL/Photo Researchers, Inc.; p. 23 NFSTC.org; pp. 30, 31 Shutterstock.com; p. 34 © Tom McHugh/ Photo Researchers, Inc.; pp. 37, 46 © Universal Images Group Limited/Alamy; p. 38 G. Wanner/ScienceFoto/Getty Images; p. 41 © AP Images; p. 44 (left) Courtesy of the University of Kansas Medical Center Archives; p. 44 (right) Wikimedia Commons; p. 48 © PHANIE/Photo Researchers, Inc.; pp. 52–53 © Biophoto Associates/ Photo Researchers, Inc.; p. 54 © Science Source/Photo Researchers, Inc.; pp. 56–57 © Dr. Jeremy Burgess/Photo Researchers, Inc.; p. 61 © A. Barrington Brown/Photo Researchers, Inc.; p. 63 © M. Wurtz/Biozentrum, University of Basel/Photo Researchers, Inc.; p. 65 Roger Tully/Stone/Getty Images; p. 67 © Martin Shields/ Photo Researchers, Inc.

Designer: Nicole Russo; Editor: Bethany Bryan; Photo Researcher: Amy Feinberg